The Power and Light that is You

A Guide to Enlightened Self Expression

Second Edition

By

Linda Lee

BALBOA.
PRESS

A DIVISION OF HAY HOUSE

Balboa Press books may be ordered through booksellers or by contacting:

Balboa Press
A Division of Hay House
1663 Liberty Drive
Bloomington, IN 47403
www.balboapress.com
1 (877) 407-4847

Because of the dynamic nature of the Internet, any web addresses or links contained in this book may have changed since publication and may no longer be valid. The views expressed in this work are solely those of the author and do not necessarily reflect the views of the publisher, and the publisher hereby disclaims any responsibility for them.

The author of this book does not dispense medical advice or prescribe the use of any technique as a form of treatment for physical, emotional, or medical problems without the advice of a physician, either directly or indirectly. The intent of the author is only to offer information of a general nature to help you in your quest for emotional and spiritual well-being. In the event you use any of the information in this book for yourself, which is your constitutional right, the author and the publisher assume no responsibility for your actions.

Cover Art by Erin Pace-Molina
Illustration by Patricia Lynne

Print information available on the last page.

ISBN: 978-1-5043-5828-6 (sc)
ISBN: 978-1-5043-5830-9 (hc)
ISBN: 978-1-5043-5829-3 (e)

Library of Congress Control Number: 2016908738

Balboa Press rev. date: 07/13/2016

Contents

Dedication

This book is dedicated to my four grandchildren Andrew, Brayden, Ellianna and Natalee. With deep hope and faith that they will be the first generation to fully live their lives consciously with love and compassion and turn the tide of the old into the magnificent new by living the Universal Laws with love, fully and freely.....

The lotus flower represents fortune in Buddhism. It grows in muddy water rising and blooming above the murk to achieve enlightenment. The colors have different symbolism as well, such as white represents purity of mind and spirit; red is compassion and love, blue is common sense and uses wisdom and logic to create enlightenment; pink represents the history and legends of Buddha; purple speaks of spirituality and mysticism and gold represents all achievements of enlightenment.

Introduction
Journey of Discovery

"What you seek is seeking you."
Rumi

I know a woman who as a child her life was more or less uneventful. She was raised in a large, religious family – and to this day, she is grateful for the spiritual foundation her family helped her create. She did face some challenges. Her family moved often, and it was too difficult for her to form relationships since she knew she would eventually leave. However, as she would learn later in life, everything has a reason for happening, and everything happened to teach her. She would learn that it all happened to prepare her for greater things in life than she could imagine.

There was also more death in her family than average; however when you have a large family the frequency of death increases with more family members, and it becomes a natural part of life. One death in particular had a profound effect: the family member, who was her paternal grandfather had cancer for a known period of less than six months. She wasn't particularly close to her grandfather, but seeing how other family members handled this situation caused her to form many new thoughts, observations and belief patterns that ultimately set her on her life's path.

Upon returning home from the funeral of her grandfather, she retired to a quiet room in darkness. With her eyes closed in contemplation soon three seemingly little questions came into her eleven-year-old mind:

1) What caused this disease?
2) How could it have been prevented?
3) Why do these thoughts frighten me?

The third question arose because these thoughts took her into a place where she had never been before. It was dark, uncharted territory and a bit scary. She asked herself, "If it's me thinking in this mind, why would I be afraid of my own thoughts and mind?" She was literally bumping up against the boundary of her consciousness and experiencing expansion of her awareness!

This question would resonate with her as she grew older. As her life unfolded she found herself learning how to live simply, making food from scratch, understanding nutrition and working in the Alternative Health field where she was exposed to and learned a myriad of holistic ways to prevent disease and support health; including an understanding and love of herbs, supplements, whole nutritious foods, and different ways of thinking and living; she became educated in several different modalities of energy work and gained understanding as to why and how we create imbalances in our lives. Then she discovered deep inner-mind work where she realized most all dis-ease and imbalance begins with our thoughts whether physical, mental, emotional or spiritual.

As many people often experience, she found the journey wasn't a straight or nicely paved road toward a destination. She found little support (if any) from others. There were those people along the way who physically, mentally and emotionally did everything possible to break her spirit and bring her to her knees; and some turned their backs entirely, which would have allowed her to forget the truth of who she was if she had allowed it. It would have been easy for her to give up. As a matter of fact there were times she thought about giving up because that would have been much easier. Yet something kept moving her toward her purpose. What was it that drove her forward? Was it her natural curiosity, excitement, joy, deep interest, or ability to follow her inner guidance? Yes, it was all of those things and more.

Yes, this story is about me, Linda Lee. I have persevered because my calling is to serve, teach and guide others. I have strived to bring this work and myself out of the darkness and into the light. I have discovered my deep inner power in the process. I want to help others realize the power and light that is not only within me, it is in all of us. If I had given up, I would be living with regret, depression, unhappiness, blame, judgment and more. None of that is worth not living your life and realizing your truth, and it would have deteriorated the quality of my life.

There is something to say about getting older. When I turned 40 I realized it was time to get busy, stop wasting time, and do what my heart told me to do. There was simply no time to waste. When I moved into my 50's it became about doing all of these things I have studied, believed and loved at a much deeper level. It was also about, maybe for the first time, learning to live my truth, be authentic, and teach what I know about playing life "full-out", leaving fear behind, and realizing what that really means. I continue to be a work in progress and I'm not sure I am here to reach perfection however, it is our duty and obligation to share our insights and wisdom with others as we are all here to assist each other on our way back home. Amazingly and gratefully the Universe has also supported all of my endeavors.

A WORD ABOUT GARDENING

One way to look at your life is like a garden and a seed. We are all like seeds planted in a garden and then shaped by the environment we're "planted" in. When we are in the womb and then born we are like seeds planted in the ground that sprout and burst forth, upward and outward. Early on we depend on others to give us the right nutrients, sunshine, hydration, positive role models, and lots of love to push up from the nurturing soil to find our own light and stand on our own with confidence, strength and courage. When we are young we may be fortunate to have those people who will tend to our personal growth in positive, loving ways. If not we may have people step on us, deprive us of light, throw dirt on us, or hinder our abilities to come into full fruition making it a difficult task. However, remember that those experiences need not define us for the rest of our lives.

Some of us are fortunate to become more aware in life and begin to understand the value and importance of our choices. We recognize that much of what happens in life can be changed by a simple choice. We might ask ourselves questions to clarify and figure out the right choices for us. Questions such as:

- How do I want to perceive this situation?
- What is right for me?

- Am I a victim?
- Am I free?
- Do I have to live the way others want me to?
- Do I have a choice?
- What good will come if I take it personally?
- Do I have time to assume it's about me?
- Am I living in my integrity?
- What would be the best I could do for myself?
- Do I honor myself?
- Do I respect myself?
- Do I love myself?

You can look at life from two different perspectives. One way is to believe deep down that what you want does not exist and is impossible to attain even if it did exist. I believe this belief system is a crime against your own infinite potential in life as you've made a choice to deny even the possibility. Or you can look at life with the understanding that life is a gift to cherish and feel gratitude toward, and all things are possible. If you see life this way, it's more likely you will make different choices about how you spend your time and ultimately shapes your life.

Unfortunately so many people live life from a place of fear. They live small and feel undeserving or unworthy, these are the two deepest wounds that most of humanity suffers from. These are the worst diseases we have on the planet and that is most of us do not feel worthy, or that you're good enough, maybe you don't feel important or you believe you just can't do what you dream to do with your life. We see it all around us. For example, I lived that way for a long period of time, and that existence and thought process could have swallowed me up had I allowed it to do so. I could have settled and remained stuck in my old thought patterns. You'll likely recognize these thoughts:

- You work a job you don't love till you die.
- You believe that you must accept your life as it is.
- You have no thought or action around infinite possibility.
- You do not have the ability to create your life.
- You are not responsible for your choices or outcomes.
- Life just happens to you.
- You are a victim.

You may believe these thought patterns are true. I am going to tell you these beliefs are limiting and not true they are simply an illusion. I wanted to write this book to illustrate something different, to help you expand your thought patterns and help you develop a broader vision so you can find your truth to expand awareness in your life. The bulleted list above is an example about the way some people see life, but these are not "truths" about me or you.

In this book, I'm going to give you a new set of tools to use to expand your awareness. You have the power within yourself to change how you feel and see your life, what you touch and believe, and how you can choose to change whatever you feel needs to change. These abilities are all simply within your grasp. With the tools provided in this book you will be guided and experience empowerment to make the right choices for you – the kind of choices that will help you realize your dreams and live the life you are here to live.

So this book is my gift to you, the person who is open to pushing the boundaries of thinking, being and breaking up the old patterns where you are stuck. Maybe you'll even decide to do what your heart is calling you to do. If not now, when?

Chapter 1
Remembering Who You Are!

As within, so without ... God is but Love, and therefore so am I. ♥
A Course In Miracles

In the beginning there was light, vibration and sound. This is energy. Simply, everything is energy. I'm going to repeat that, <u>everything</u> is energy.

First of all, we are all amazing human beings. **You** are an amazing human being. We have literally come to this planet to experience all we are here to experience and so much more. We are here to learn and grow and expand our awareness using the five senses we were born with and to **remember** the other senses that are less obvious or unknown and to claim them. What would life be like if we did not have purpose sprinkled with lots of love? The fact is if we are not growing and expanding we are stagnant and dying. Many experience life without purpose and little sense of what love truly is. Most have allowed ego to run their lives. Little happiness or freedom can be found with these limiting perspectives.

Science has looked into the cosmos and discovered the way the structure of the cosmos looks. The macrocosm (the world and the universe considered as a single entity) in appearance seems to be the same as the structure of the cellular appearance of the brain, which is a microcosm (a miniature world or universe, in this case within our body). We are made up of the same elements of the cosmos and the planet we live on. For instance, our planet is made up of approximately 70 percent water and so are we. Furthermore, the Earth's magnetic resonances vibrate at the same frequency as our heart rhythms and brain waves. It's also said that 90 percent of our body mass is made up of stardust and contains all of the same elements except hydrogen and helium. So these interesting discoveries are proof that we are made up of the same stuff of the universe and the planet we inhabit!

As this being a certain truth, then we may see ourselves as gods and goddesses of the universe we call our bodies, the microcosm. We have complete control of this body by how we treat it, what habits we choose to entertain, our actions, thoughts we think, and what we surround our body with whether cosmetically, clothing, your environment, even the food you put into it. Do you surround your miraculous being with love and treat it as the temple it is that houses your soul and spirit. Do you treat it as well as your vehicle in the driveway, the body that helps us move through this life? How do you honor this responsibility? If you have given the power of choice away to someone or something else you may be feeling disempowered in life, and you may also be experiencing illness or "dis-ease" and not knowing why or asking yourself why me.

Did you know that **uni-verse** means **one song**? Isn't that beautiful? This is significant because if we are of the universe which is of God, Source, Spirit or whatever your terminology is for what is greater than your self or **All That Is,** would that not mean that you are the same or at least have similar qualities as this energy? And if you are the same as this energy would you not have the same capabilities and even abilities that this energy represents? This unique energy represents unlimited potential in all areas of your life, including love, abundance, prosperity, creativity, joy, abundance and whatever you can dream in your life.

In my experiences with clients I have worked with is that the further separated they feel from what we call God or Higher Self the more feelings of fear, anxiety, depression, uselessness, unworthiness, hopelessness and undeserving they have felt and experienced. I feel my work is to help my clients reconnect to their highest source of energy and help them remember they are empowered, and they are a beautiful light to shine out into the world. The *Course in Miracles* states that if it is not of love it is fear. Two types of energy cannot occupy the same space. So if you could choose a God that is of fear, damnation, judgment or punishment as opposed to a God of unconditional love, joy, unlimited possibility and more, what is your choice? Which God is worthy of your precious energy?

Which belief system do you choose? What does that feel like? What are your limitations around your choice if any or what does it stir up for you? Again, two types of energy cannot occupy the same space, just like two cars cannot occupy the same parking space. Those people who do not have a connection to a higher power or are feeling so unworthy they believe they can't even have that relationship or it's completely inaccessible to them are the most lost. Feeling separation from your Higher Self leads to addiction, unhealthy relationships, poor choices in life, and overall unhappiness.

A WORD ABOUT FEAR

We cannot condemn fear entirely or invalidate it. Without fear we would have no measure as to where we are at in our consciousness expansion. For example, just a few years ago I would have never sought out the experience of speaking in public. I was just too fearful. Under what circumstance would I ever want to do such a thing? It seemed difficult to even consider. I also had plenty of support to stay stuck in that belief system. When I decided this was my next step I looked at my fear, pushed through it, and created and accepted opportunities to speak, which was definitely out of my comfort zone yet that is where all growth ocurrs.

Fear is a gauge for where we are in our lives. If it's something worth pushing through to the next step we must *"step away from the fear"* in order to expand beyond our self-limiting boundaries. Fear allows contrast – without fear we may not understand love, joy or happiness because we would have no measure of what it isn't.

Another example of why we need fear is to keep us safe from danger and situations that are not for our highest good. We need an element of fear because when fear comes up it has a message for us to make loving decisions for our selves, which help us grow and expand beyond where we're at or to keep us safe. Fear is useful as long as it doesn't overcome your life and paralyze you into non-action, stagnation, isolation through drugs (legal or not) or alcohol, or create complacent and unproductive relationships.

I believe we need a certain amount of fear at least for now on this planet – that is until we are able to create a safe, loving and fully supportive life that is in complete harmony with our self and our higher values, families, communities and the planet. In other words:

Heaven on Earth. Evolving beyond a world of duality and finding unity with one another and the planet. Until then, utilize that bit of fear for yourself to understand the contrast it provides to help you realize when you may be moving into uncharted territory to grow and expand or if something is amiss that needs to have your attention to keep you safe. Remember fear always has a lesson, and that is to make a loving decision for yourself.

BLACK HOLE OR BRIGHT STAR?

I had a realization in my early 20's (maybe it was all the *Carl Sagan* I was watching at the time): I asked myself looking out into the cosmos, would I rather be a black hole or shine like the brightest star I could imagine? I decided, of course, the brightest star I could imagine. I wanted to shine like the brightest star not collapse into darkness or nothingness. I also believed that was what I was here to do: increase my vibration to be all I could be and to honor this gift of life. How I believed this could be achieved was to be the best person and version of myself I could be, honor my body, grow spiritually, learn and experience all I could, treat others as I would like to be treated, give, serve others, be healthy, be an example for others and more.

As I began to grow in my awareness I realized taking care of my body, mind and spirit honors those gifts and allows me to live my purpose. If we don't have our health there is no way to achieve all we desire in life, period. The most important components to health in my opinion are: a) to have a flexible spine, b) consume a clean, healthy diet and water, c) practice deep breathing daily, d) get regular movement/exercise every day, e) keep the digestive system healthy thereby creating a clean colon, f) enjoy the sunshine and g) get regular, deep sleep. Health is our wealth!

A side note about the phenomenon of a black hole. A black hole is what is left behind after a star has collapsed. It can also be seen spiritually as a portal to other levels of existence which can offer new insights and knowledge – that is, if we choose to learn the lessons that took us to that place of darkness. Moving through these times in our lives allows us to learn, discover new ways of thinking, expand awareness, and gain new insights if we simply choose to contemplate why certain situations or experiences may have shown up for us to experience. All we experience is part of our journey for our highest good and is here to serve us in that pursuit. There is always time to make another choice. All can lead to new insights and understandings if we choose to see them.

Science and quantum physics has also proved that all beings and things, *all energy* has a vibration. We each have our own vibration. Health vibrates at a certain level and sickness vibrates at another level. We all know what that feels like right? We all have gone into a room where we want to immediately go the other direction; and we've all been in a room that we never want to leave, it just simply feels good to be there. The point is some will say "energy" is "woo-woo," however these people only believe in some types of energy yet other kinds are off-limits. They may believe in electricity, microwave, radio or the miracle of conception, they know they think and have emotions but cannot touch them (although we cannot explain how these technically work or can see it we just accept them) yet they don't believe in the idea that simply everything is energy, and we are all beings of energy or the unseen or intangible.

Just because we can't explain something does not mean it is not valid or exists on some level. There is a story in the *Bible* about those who went to Jesus for healing and believed if they just touched Jesus' robe they would be healed. What happened energetically is that these people who aligned themselves energetically with Jesus were healed. Jesus told them, "Your faith has made you well" (Matthew 9:22). What does this say to us? Jesus literally told these people that if they didn't trust or believe that they could be healed just by touching his robe healing would not have happened.

Faith defined is "unquestioning belief". So to what degree do we unquestioningly believe we are abundant, prosperous, surrounded by love, creative, whole, healthy, and perfect as we are right now? Do you believe you are made from the same stuff as your Creator? If Jesus is the Son of God do you believe you are a child of that same God? If the answer is yes why do you believe you do not have the same capabilities as Jesus or Buddha such as unbounded love, self-healing, happiness or abundance?

The point to all of this is how far our awareness or our boundaries are around who we are versus an "enlightened being". What limits have you placed on yourself? The truth is we are all on our way to enlightenment and reawakening we are just in varying degrees of growth and change whether we are conscious of it or not. It's time to claim who you are and begin to live your life accordingly. Can you imagine the changes we could make living from the higher principles most of us say we believe in yet in this moment in time we only have excuses for not truly living what we say we actually believe.

How separate do you allow yourself to be from this energy? The less you can relate to our sameness or oneness with this enlightened being or any other enlightened being who has walked or is walking this planet now is the degree to which you may feel separated and are suffering.

In John 14:12 it says, "The truth is, anyone who believes in me will do the same works I have done and even greater works …" We are literally being told that when we "believe" in who we are we can do the same things Jesus did and more. He didn't even demonstrate to us all of his capabilities which are also ours! So I use these illustrations to ask you how far you believe in the power and light that is you? How are you standing in your way? For what reasons are you holding yourself back? What limited thinking are you using to play small shrinking your light within?

Marianne Williamson said it best in her book A Return To Love:

"Our deepest fear is not that we are inadequate. Our deepest fear is that we are powerful beyond measure. It is our light, not our darkness that most frightens us. We ask ourselves, Who am I to be brilliant, gorgeous, talented, fabulous? Actually, who are you not to be? You are a child of God. Your playing small does not serve the world. There is nothing enlightened about shrinking so that other people won't feel insecure around you. We are all meant to shine, as children do. We were born to make manifest the glory of God that is within us. It's not just in some of us; it's in everyone. And as we let our own light shine, we unconsciously give other people permission to do the same. As we are liberated from our own fear, our presence automatically liberates others."

You were not born with thoughts of limitation, these are learned thought patterns from generations of struggle, lack and forgetting who you are. You only need to remember unlimited possibility is your birthright, so begin to shift your perception so you can make amazing changes in your life.

You are unique. You have special and unique gifts. No one can do it (whatever that is for you) the way you can. Play full-out and out loud. Lisa Nichols said: (paraphrased) it's time to be who you are, shine bright, don't allow anyone to dim your light, if someone can't handle your light give them sunglasses! I say, live out loud; be the creative force in your own life and amazing things will begin to happen in your life.

Chapter 2
Do You Know Your True Inner Power?

"A mind that is stretched by new thoughts can never go back to its old dimensions."
unknown

Do you really know your true inner power? When you look around are you happy with what you've created? Do you take accountability for your creation? Do you believe you've created what you see around you? If you believe in that power to create, what does it feel like? What would it feel like if you've not yet experienced or acknowledged that feeling or empowerment? Take a moment to reflect on your personal thoughts around this subject.

Since recent books have emerged and been embraced on the market (e.g., *The Secret*) many people seeking to expand their state of mind have embraced popular concepts such as using the Law of Attraction to create the life you want. These laws help us to understand concepts like abundance, prosperity thinking and gratitude. Yet at the same time people get excited about these ideas and outwardly try to apply the concepts yet many people try and fail. They will throw their arms up in frustration and falsely believe things like, "Well, it doesn't work for me. I thought about only checks arriving in my mailbox, and I still got bills."

What is not understood is that it's one thing to think you understand a powerful yet simple concept like the Law of Attraction, but it is another thing to apply it and make it work in your own life.

THE POWER OF UNQUESTIONING
BELIEF: KNOW WHAT YOU KNOW

Ways you can achieve a deep sense of knowing:

- Trust yourself
- Know who you are
- Trust the process of life
- Practice Gratitude (this opens you to more)
- Practice quieting the mind ~ you have all the answers, this is the art of listening
- Trust you are being guided at all times for your highest good and purposes in life
- Know there is a Power greater than yourself
- Live with Joy and Purpose

These things take practice. For many of us it's taken decades to get to the point to even ask the question of how to begin this process. Be patient and loving with yourself in this process, it will get easier and easier for you.

These same people often believe they are in control of their lives. While they like the idea and concept of things like applying a prosperity consciousness and creating abundance, they do what is suggested yet still don't have all the tools to apply it. Many times we only know or fully accept a concept at the intellectual level and we never get to the point of being able to create with what we *know*. We think we know, we don't know that we know. Then life may reflect something much different than what was expected. Where did we go wrong?

The answer is simple. We have not integrated our knowledge with **unquestioning belief**. We have not integrated the information into experience by feeling and knowing it to be so. Literally merging our knowingness and our senses into one, we are in the vortex of creation. When you can merely think it and it's so, you know you are in that natural energy of creating, there is no longer a space between the thought and the creation. That space between is where ego and old programming gets involved and sabotages your creation with all its analysis, questions, belittling, you know.

If you are one of these people and you want to change, it's time to recognize it. You are probably still thinking that you know and not truly knowing that you know. You may even harbor a belief system with feelings of unworthiness and undeserving because of a "consciousness of lack," which blocks you and holds you back from what you truly desire in life. This is not uncommon however, it's still an old thought pattern that most likely goes back to the beginning of time somewhere which no longer serves you. It is imperative to remove the blocks around this old habit pattern of thinking to break through what binds you from the growth and expansion you desire in life no matter what area of your life this holds you back in. It could even reflect in several areas of your life.

CASE STUDY – SELF-ESTEEM AND CONFIDENCE-BUILDING

For example, I worked with a client who came to me because she suffered with self-esteem issues and lack of confidence. She wanted to become a public speaker. As details unfolded she was struggling in her business. She couldn't understand why she was unable to get her clients to agree to work with her. Her closing rate was dismal.

She realized she was judging her potential clients at the outset as to whether they could afford her services or were even truly interested at all in what she had to offer. Now remember that we cannot receive more than we are ready to receive from others and others will reflect back to us our belief system so we can look at it and learn from it if we choose to see it. She also isolated herself and was very quiet in public for the most part and cared deeply about what others thought of her. This thought alone will paralyze you from ever getting in front of a lot of people to share your message and will hold you back in lots of different ways! When the realization was made that when you judge others you judge yourself, and that when you let go of what others think of you, you have much more time to create all you desire from your heart. Once she made this realization everything changed for her. Her business is now flourishing, and she is reaching out to speak more in public and share her knowledge and expertise in a more dynamic way and *'stepped away from fear'*.

CASE STUDY – NAIL-BITING PROBLEM SOLVED

Another client, who had a severe nail-biting problem and also felt weighed down by past relationships, came to me for assistance. She dealt with frustration from childhood that was buried so deep there was no way for her to know this was at the core. When this was broken through everything changed for her. She became fully committed to her current relationship and cut her fingernails for the first time she could ever remember in her 30 years of life! Amazing what clearing old baggage we don't even know we're carrying can do in your life.

NO LIMITS

I have worked with several clients who were unemployed, wanted to change jobs, find there life purpose, or were lacking a prosperity consciousness. When your thinking is limited in a way that you only accept a certain criteria of possibilities (such as a financial depression or recession), we begin to believe as the masses believe:

- The right job does not exist for me.
- People don't have money for my service.
- It will take a very long time to find any job.
- There aren't enough jobs.
- I will suffer or my family will suffer.
- I don't have enough money, experience, worthiness, etc.
- I have to work hard for money.
- I cannot live my dream, I'll starve.
- I can only make a certain amount of money.
- I will never have the luxury of living my dream job or work.

These are examples of mass hypnosis based on negative thinking. Allow yourself to *'step away from fear'* and instead trust your deep inner voice that is always nudging you in the direction of your heart's desire. It will never lead you astray.

A WORD ABOUT MONEY

Money is simply energy. The flow of money in and out of your life is basically a manifestation of how you feel about money. Money is just a thing. We give money meaning. If you hold onto and hoard money as if it will never again come into your life, or we become fearful of not having enough, this thinking will simply stop the flow of money coming into your life. When we trust that money will always be there with trust and gratitude somehow it miraculously always is, and it opens us to more.

Money is a demonstration of how we feel inside. What do your outer conditions say to you about how you feel? Do you feel abundant and prosperous? Do you feel you have to work hard for money? Why doesn't it grow on trees anyway? These are all old programming. When we remove the blocks around lack we can open the spigot of more into our life and create a natural flow of releasing and receiving. Ask yourself 'How can I open to receive more'?

There is a spiritual law, a Universal Law called "tithing". This is a direct way to demonstrate you have moved away from lack and moved toward the knowledge you will always be provided for and that there is enough. It has been used since the beginning of time and works. There are also other ways to give as well, like your treasures, your time and worthy causes that you have given thoughtful consideration to and are in alignment with your values and is for the greater good.

Remember the garden? If you try to water your garden and you stand on the water hose you block the abundance of water that is yours. By allowing the water to flow fully and freely in order to water the garden fully you reap the fruits of your labor and your garden will grow to full fruition. Money is not good or evil; money is merely what we have decided it is and believe it is. You do not have to believe all you have been programmed for. You are the only one thinking thoughts in your head, no one else. If you believe money is evil it is, if you believe money is good and provides wonderful things in life it does. Either way you are right. Change your thinking; change your life!

Your reality is created by the power and intention of your thoughts. Look around you again. Could there be some improvement? Are you standing in your own way to truly create all you desire in life? If the answer is yes there is still work to do.

BE YOUR OWN PERSONAL MAGICIAN

What is a magician? It is an extraordinarily skilled and powerful person! Claim this for yourself. What can you do to achieve this?

- Love yourself and others unconditionally; we are all in this together.
- Wake up loving your life everyday!
- Practice forgiveness, it will free you.
- Find what inspires you to make a difference in life for you and others.
- Gain control of your thoughts; you are the thinker no one else, you have a choice.
- Realize all is energy, and therefore you are connected to all you desire to create.
- Visualize every day what you want to create in your life.
- Practice prayer, it is the art of asking for what you desire.
- Practice contemplation and/or meditation each day, this is the art of listening, all of the answers already lie within you.
- Practice releasing all negativity and fear. It is not of service to you. (utilize tools in upcoming chapters)
- Ask, Believe, Receive

Say "Abracadabra' a lot! It's Hebrew for "I create what I speak!"

The power of choice is yours!

Your thought and habit patterns are creating for you and usually on the side of comfortable decisions no matter what level of pain you have mentally, physically or emotionally and it's meant to keep you safe because it's easy and you know that place best.

The unknown is frightening to most people. It may even hold varying degrees of pain yet you allow yourself to be held captive. These thoughts are not who you truly are. Your deep inner spirit knows you are more than these thoughts and only sees you as unlimited. It's time to no longer allow these negative thought patterns to run your life!

You are literally a magician creating your reality thought by thought, belief by belief. Thoughts affect your health physically, mentally, emotionally and spiritually, and emanate outward to your family, friends, community and ultimately all beings on the planet. It's time to clear old ways of thinking and being in order to live life from the highest-level possible. The old ways are no longer working. It's time to make changes for a more harmonious way of living.

Remember it will take practice to become aware and to begin the process of pulling the weeds from the garden of your mind so the beauty of who you are can truly flourish and overcome the old ways of thinking. The tools within the upcoming chapters will be of great use if you are only open to utilizing them to find your innate power, increasing your vibration thereby releasing the light within to shine brighter and brighter without hindrance outward to effect all beings we come in contact with and more.

"My will is the instrument of the image of God within me. In my will lies the limitless power that controls all the forces of nature. As I am made in God's image, that power is mine to bring about whatever I desire."

Parmahansa Yogananda

Chapter 3
The Power of Thought

"The mind is everything.
What you think you become."
Buddha

I live in the country off of a dirt road. As I drove this familiar road one day (a road I take most every day), a road with all its twists and turns, it became an enchanting metaphor for me. Actually this road was once a part of the Pony Express Trail in the Sierra Foothills. I pictured people walking or riding their horses in days gone by along this road with all of their hopes and dreams swirling in their minds and hearts just like people do now.

Intention is like a road in the country; once there was no road, but when many people walked and rode horses or wagons on this bumpy road someone had the thought and then a visualization of how life could be easier, and eventually the paved road came into existence along with motorized vehicles. When you consciously direct the neurological pathways (the thoughts in your mind) with high level thoughts, carefully choosing each thought, these thoughts create new pathways that are light, fluid pathways with every supporting thought. When you consciously employ this thought process then you are in the driver's seat. You no longer behave in ways based on old programming.

The new pathways you consciously create will take you right where you want to go and create loving pathways for all you desire in life, which allows flexibility for change and greater awareness in the future.

When you continue to think the way you've always thought, especially when thoughts are negative and not serving you, your neurological pathways become deeply grooved like an old dirt road with gullies and big blocks in the way that hinder your progress making it difficult to see new ways of thinking and being – you're simply on automatic no matter how much pain you're in. You are literally a prisoner of your thoughts. Being a prisoner of your thoughts and beliefs causes physical issues, mental and emotional issues and stops your spiritual expansion. The good news is you can actually change your thought processes and "re-pave" the road your on to take you somewhere new if you simply choose something different. You are not stuck with how you've been programmed to think. Much like a dirt road that can be deeply grooved by continual travel or weather, you can actually recreate that roadway, reconstruct, and redirect it to make life a smoother, more positive experience.

"As certainly as acorns always become oak trees,
the thoughts you think become your reality."
Dr. Mo

RULES OF HOW THE MIND AND THOUGHTS WORK

- Your thoughts are real and take shape and form.
- Your mind is continually receiving information and sending information out.
- Your thoughts and mind affect not only your internal self, they affect everything around you.
- The Law of Attraction works as each thought magnetizes like thoughts continually creating either positive or negative in your life.
- You have the power to either keep your thoughts or release them.
- You can only think one thought at a time giving you the ability to easily become discerning.
- Remember that we are connected to not only the inner world; we are connected to the outer world.
- You either attract or repel with how you think.
- You have the ability to think the thoughts you choose by changing thoughts to serve you in more positive ways.
- What you think over and over again will take root whether positive or negative.
- It only takes two minutes per day of focus to change your neuropathways!
- You don't have to believe everything you think.

EMPOWERING YOUR THOUGHT PROCESS

Here's how it works. Everything begins with a thought. Thoughts are incoming information that exists within the mind in the form of a concept, idea, information or feeling. Simply put, *Thoughts lead to feelings - Feelings lead to actions - Actions lead to results.* As you may already know up until age seven we literally absorb everything around us. We have no discerning ability or way to filter incoming information;

we just accept it as truth. It's not until the age of eight that we begin to have the ability to think more about incoming information mostly in the form of observations about how others behave and speak to one another. Eighty percent of our programming was done by the age of eight years old! So as adults we are making important choices about our lives from this 80-percent download and early conditioning that we've already accepted as truth. Unless we take action by observing our thoughts and habit patterns and realizing most of what we believe to be true isn't even our own thoughts (you may hear your mother's voice, father's, grandparents, church leaders, school teachers any other authority figure as a child that made an impact), we need to be proactive and change what we need to according to our personal truth and highest good in life.

Unless you challenge your belief system from time to time you may not truly know if they're your beliefs or someone else's. Unless you take action instead of blindly accepting what you believe is your truth, or your own thoughts and beliefs, you will continually adapt and build these patterns year after year thereafter, kind of like building on a shaky foundation. Whatever we experience henceforth we begin to attach meaning and value which become beliefs. These ways of thinking are essentially based on that 80-percent foundation of core beliefs that were developed in those first eight years of life. Thereafter we continue to attach meaning and value to experiences which become our beliefs, and then it becomes solidified further with emotions. These feelings cause you to behave in a certain way and produce results, which manifest in your life according to those beliefs. Is there something in your life not working and you can't understand why it continues to happen over and over again?

Now let's apply our thought process to my original garden metaphor. Your thoughts are like "seeds" (feelings), which are really perceived sensations, and these sensations are the "soil" that nourish the "seeds" and give your thoughts meaning. Emotions power-up feelings and sensations and cause a strong surge, which produces a result or condition in your life, becoming belief.

For example, another client came from a home of incredible abuse. These are difficult situations that deeply program children's lives. In this particular instance the relationship she has with her parents is deeply enmeshed even after more than 60 years. How this has affected her adult life is it has resulted in negative outcomes in most, if not all of her relationships, she's been divorced many times, unable to find fulfilling relationships, has issues with extreme control, is very blunt and has difficulty being soft and vulnerable. Who can blame her? With help in removing old thought patterns and blocks attributed to this abuse she now experiences more of a flow in life, a softer heart, and kinder outlook on life. She has noticed the change yet it's still a long road to healing completely, and she is on her way.

Remember you create every moment through your thoughts and feelings whether you are conscious of your choices or not. Even when you are not conscious, there is no excuse to ignore the conditions you've created out of ignorance. Remember blame is not constructive so whatever you've created, you can create something new. Stop blaming and become empowered! It is time now to become more aware in order to make changes. Yes, it will take practice. Most of us have not been taught the power of our minds; it's not taught in school or from our family yet this should be on the top of the list of what is taught to us! The powers that be don't want you to realize your own capabilities, power or light as you would no longer be under their control. My philosophy is that as soon as you awaken to your true inner power and light, you will begin to live your life from your higher truths. Truths that support higher spiritual values, and the value of each human being from a place of love, integrity and honor for self, community, all living creatures, and this beautiful planet we call home. Imagine this kind of world for a moment …

In the forthcoming chapters, I'm going to teach you how to not only to change the thoughts that no longer serve you, but also to harness the power of your thoughts to live the life you dream of living and create all you desire. What if you begin to live your life right now exactly how you've always pictured it?

THE "I CAN'T BEGIN NOW" LIST

Here is a list of some potential reasons why in your mind you can't live the life of your dreams. Make your own list of what is holding you back so you can see them.

- I have too many responsibilities to live my dream.
- I don't have enough money.
- My family won't understand or let me.
- I'm not talented enough.
- I'm not good enough.
- I don't have the right appearance.
- I don't have enough time.
- I'm not worthy or deserving.

Now make a list of how to break through what is holding you back.

- I don't really need cable TV or two cars to survive.
- I am responsible for myself, no one makes decisions for me.

- I am worthy and deserving of all I desire.
- Time is valuable, and it's up to me to use it in the most positive way for myself.
- I am perfect just as I am.
- I have everything I need to live my life to its fullest now!

First you may want to list all of the real or imagined reasons you cannot begin right now just to get them out of the way once and for all.

Then take a look at the "I-can't" list. Those reasons don't feel really good or supportive do they? Okay so you see them, it's now time to get rid of them. Take the list and ceremoniously burn it. Get a fire-safe container in a fire-safe area and light the paper on fire to release all those imagined blocks forever. As you see them go up in smoke, see all of these excuses blow away in the breeze, back into the nothingness from where they came. Take your breakthrough list and place where you can see it everyday! Let these become your mantras and remember it is your birth right to be happy and prosperous, claim it for yourself now!

Belief is simply something you have told yourself over and over again and makes you responsible for your experience in life. Remember you can change your belief, and you have the power to change your experience. You are the only one thinking in your mind, and you have the ability to change what it is that no longer works for you by merely making another choice which changes your mind.

*"A belief system is nothing more than a thought
you've thought over and over again."*
~ Wayne Dyer

Do you believe that if you change your mind you change your world? It's true if you believe it; it's true if you don't! Either way you're creating.

A WORD ABOUT SELF-AFFIRMATIONS

I love affirmations. However, the problem is if you haven't taken care of the inner work say around something like money and you are saying an affirmation such as "I have $1 million in the bank now." You may find another little (or big) voice from the back saying, "Yeah right, you wish, this will never work" (ego), which defeats you and you give up before you've even really begun. Even if the affirmations begin to work it could take a very long time until you break down all the ego has to say first about all that illusion(ego) and all the blocks and obstacles around it.

My recommendation is to attain a qualified hypnotherapist such as myself to assist you in removing the blocks you have around money (or anything else for that matter) and all that old programming that says you're not worthy, good enough, or deserving to have what you desire in your bank account or any aspect of your life you'd like to align better with, whether it's relationships, your geography, the people around you or whatever you dream of.

Once this occurs you can begin your journey to attain your goal without the negative chatter telling you can't have what you desire. You will have tools to move through it. Affirmations will then work quicker and help you be more clear to help you stay on track.

Remember that affirmations must be realistic, you can always up the game as you go along. However, start within reason and grow with your confidence as you make the changes, goals and desires you are creating.

"We cannot be prepared for something while secretly believing it will not happen."
Nelson Mandela

RULES REGARDING AFFIRMATIONS

- Make your affirmation short, sweet and simple such as "I am happy and at peace now."
- It must always be positive, attainable and in the NOW.
- Will, for the most part, be said internally.
- You don't have to believe your affirmation and never force yourself to believe it. Simply trust the process, trust yourself.
- Remember that simple repetition will allow a natural process of healing the old negative thought patterns.
- When stating your affirmation, allow yourself to feel it and see it already as a reality in your life.
- Affirm health, love, prosperity, abundance and anything else you can imagine, each and every day.
- Begin doing affirmations for as little as 16 seconds and build up to 2-5 minutes at a time.
- Recognize and release any negative thoughts that may appear during this process effortlessly. See the negative thoughts simply float by with nonattachment or you can utilize the **White Light Technique** found in a later chapter that can also help with release.

Thoughts are deeply ingrained, and it takes conscious awareness, clarity, and a desire to clear out the rubbish and weeds so you can remember and hear your deep inner voice of wisdom. By the way, the best kept secret is that the deep inner voice of wisdom that emanates from the subconscious mind literally holds all the answers you seek. The good news is that when the rubbish is cleared out, that old stuff that keeps you stuck in what generations before have merely accepted as their voice, and their truths about their selves and about life and now yours, can be transformed to new ways of thinking and being. It's time to finally hear your authentic voice and realize who you truly are.

The power of thought is your most valuable tool especially when you add conscious intent. You can make amazing strides in growth, which results in more happiness, balance, and healthy control of your life with your emotions, boundaries and more.

Chapter 4
The Power of Words

"Words have power. They ignite spiritual forces that influence the events and circumstances of our lives."
Yehuda Berg

Many of us are beginning to understand the power of our words. Did you know words also have the power to create around us, inwardly and outwardly? They have the power to change relationships, change the molecular structure of our food, affect digestion, start wars, end wars, spread love or hatred, and so much more.

Science estimates that people respond to word stimuli within one- to two-tenths of a second! This is very powerful. Words are a very slow way of communicating; the energy and intent of the words will arrive before the sound of the words and are already evoking a response. It is time we harness the amazing power we have of communication for building and creating the world we all truly desire.

When you speak, whether out loud or inside your own head, the universe is listening inwardly and outwardly. If you are wishing ill onto someone those thoughts will only be heard in your head not the others, which affects you not them much more. The vibration of those ill thoughts will emanate outward from you which means you may have lost a friend, however the biggest damage will be done to you internally not them. I've heard it said that anger is like taking poison and expecting it to hurt someone else! Remember you create every moment with every thought whether you are aware or not. Ignorance does not count and not making a conscious choice does not count – you're still creating.

Early in my life I came to the realization that when we generate personal vibration or light by living our lives from the highest place possible and doing our best to honor this gift of life, it generates more light and a higher vibration. Isn't that what energy does? Like attracts like and more of the same. A simple concept but not always easy...... We're here to do our best.

I was introduced to an amazing fellow named Dr. Masaru Emoto in a movie called *What the Bleep? Down the Rabbit Hole*. Dr. Emoto did amazing experiments where he sang, spoke and surrounded water crystals with the written word or letters, pictures, music, and/or prayed into the water, then he flash-froze the water molecules.

Hado (rhymes with shadow) and literally means wave and movement. This definition is how Dr. Emoto describes the phenomenon, which led him to a series of remarkable discoveries that pertained to the nature of water. Hado is the intrinsic vibration pattern at the atomic level in all matter, which is the smallest unit of energy. Its basis is the energy of human consciousness and the root of the universe according to Dr. Emoto.

Hado creates words. Words are vibrations of nature, and therefore beautiful words create beautiful nature, ugly words create ugly. The water crystals that were surrounded with beautiful high-vibration words like love, thanks, gratitude all had beautiful symmetrical, brilliant white color, and some even had gold hues. The negative vibrations were dingy yellow and disjointed, very unpleasing to the eye. With regard to the molecular structure of water, our intent (thoughts), words, ideas and music have a profound healing or destructive effect on water.

Great work has been done by people like Karol Truman and Louise Hay who have done extensive work on how the body is affected by emotion, both positive and negative. Because we are energetic beings and thoughts are energetic there is a cause and effect by the thoughts we choose or unconsciously don't choose. Remember, we are not parts and pieces, we are intricately connected human beings; and all we say, do, experience and believe is all expressed either physically, mentally, emotionally or spiritually. We all know that love and joy sends us soaring. These are examples of high vibration health giving emotions. When we experience or express negative emotions for long periods of time, the following effects can happen to our bodies:

- Angry words and thoughts weaken the liver
- Grief weakens the lungs
- Worry weakens the heart and the brain
- Stress weakens every system in the body
- Fear weakens the kidneys
- Negativity weakens the immune system

Remember if we are 70-percent water, and we have repetitive thoughts or habit patterns or programming from the early ages of 0-8 we are literally solidifying health or imbalances in the body just like the ice crystals. Ultimately it means that what we think creates our reality not just emotionally, mentally or spiritually, it affects us physically. Since the planet is also 70-percent water this could also have profound implications for the environment. Could this mean that we could "think" polluted streams clean again or even heal the planet?

Experiments have been done in Japan with Dr. Emoto's work where 300 people, who were usually led by someone proficient in meditation (e.g., a Buddhist monk), gathered around a polluted stream. They performed a focused healing on the water for approximately one hour. According to eyewitnesses the water became visibly clearer approximately 15 minutes after the meditation. If this is indeed the case, the possibilities are endless as to what we could collectively do to clean up the environment. Just imagine the possibilities …

Many of you may be familiar with the Washington D.C. Crime Study from the summer of 1993. A Transcendental Meditation crime prevention project in Washington showed a maximum 23.3% drop in violent crime. About 173 TM Sidhas participated in meditating over a 23 day period. Before the project the Chief of Police had exclaimed that the only thing that would create a 20% drop in crime would be 20 inches of snow. The TM crime prevention project took place during blistering summer weather and exceeded the predicted 20% prediction!

As you assimilate more and more the power that is you, it won't be long before you realize that you are already abundant and prosperous. In the end, it's up to you to create and believe it with unquestioning belief and trust in yourself. You have to know that you know, not just think that you think that you know, that you can create anything you desire in your life.

A WORD ABOUT SELF-ACCEPTANCE

I would have to say that many people sadly and simply do not trust who they are! Learn to love and trust who you are by listening to that still-small voice within you. This is not ego-based behavior. You have to believe that your inner guidance will never lead you astray or off your path. Look within, we just need to be open to it and then trust who we are and trust that still-small voice, it's real. It's just that simple.

When you are able to fully accept and embrace who you are, you will understand and give yourself credit by knowing you are doing your best in this world. You can then release self-judgment, allowing yourself to learn from the next situation, always striving to make your life better on all levels and being more conscious about what your best is. Maya Angelou said it best, "When you *know* better you do better."

When we know we are doing our best we can accept others with the knowledge they are doing their best as well. Then we will cease to take things personally or make assumptions about what others may be thinking or feeling about us – and to do otherwise takes up far too much of our precious time. We will begin to live our lives with more quality, substance and integrity. Integrity is important if you want to trust yourself, it's what we do when no one is watching. When we are in full integrity, our word is all important, to our self and to others, and we begin the process of trusting our self more and more. We will learn the deep meaning of what this all truly means as we live it. We do these things because we deserve to live this way and are worthy of it; it is your birthright. We are simply here to live our purpose in the highest way possible.

It is your birthright and mine to live from our hearts, choosing happiness, abundance and harmony in life. The most important thing in life is to stop saying, "I wish" and "if only" and to start to believe that nothing is impossible (I'm possible) – and in fact all is possible and even probable. Amazing things can then begin to happen in your life because you will be aware of the possibility and observant to the seemingly little miracles that will begin to happen every day of your life more and more.

GOSSIP IS THE POISON WE SPREAD

I want to address gossip for a moment. When we speak about others behind their backs, we spread poison. When a person gossips (whether it's true or not) he or she spreads information through his or her own filters about that person. So what you say may or may not be true. Furthermore, the person who speaks ill of another is doing so out of his or her own insecurity because he or she is looking for support from others against the other person. He or she feels justified if he or she can get others to support his or her negative views. Then he or she can begin to feel like one of the group and give himself or herself a false sense of being better than or part of.

When we see gossip for what it really is, a simple desire to cause pain or harm to another the purpose of gossip becomes rather shallow. Ultimately what we feel about another is simply a reflection of ourselves and a mirror being held up to take a look at ourselves so we can then choose to make better choices or not. Remember, when you live your life from higher values you will realize that whatever it was that happened is not your business or responsibility to judge. Focus on the important things you are here to do in life, course correct if something has occurred and move on.

Let it go. There is simply no time in life to waste in this pursuit. There is no one you can change except yourself and your perceptions – this is task enough in this life. You will realize that it will empower you and unburden you as well. This is a gift you can give to yourself with practice and awareness. We need to get back to living and speaking with integrity and becoming more aligned with our highest values and standards.

ACTIVITIES TO RAISE YOUR VIBRATION

- Pray, the art of asking for your desires.
- Meditate, the art of listening for answers.
- Open to all you desire and greater things!
- Focus on your breath, in and out, this is your connection to life.
- Repeat a mantra such as "I Am Love!" or "I am Peace."
- Guard your thoughts carefully.
- Write your feelings down on paper and pour them out until you can think of nothing else to write – release.
- Know you are abundant and prosperous now!
- Practice gratitude
- Practice empathy and compassion
- Serve others

How do you increase your vibration? Begin to think more positive thoughts, love yourself and others, and show joy, gratitude, abundance, prosperity and confidence. Then align yourself with the Universal

Energy of the Divine Spirit and realize you have all the infinite possibility of what you can imagine. When you do these things, you will begin to vibrate at a higher rate and there is no stopping you! If you choose to constrict your energy, play small or give up, you begin to weaken, so will your body and vibration.

Let your light shine ... if not now when?

Chapter 5
The Power of Discernment

"The cells in your body listen and act on everything that your mind says!"

I was watching *Cat in the Hat Knows a Lot About That* with my two-year-old granddaughter one morning. I wasn't really paying too close attention to it. I was just enjoying cuddling with my sweet Natalee. All of a sudden out of the corner of my eye a rather large snake comes slithering down from the top of a tree and says: **"When you learn to quiet your mind, the world comes to you!"** "My goodness," I thought, "what a wonderful message to be sending to young children (and a good reminder for me too)!"

Our busy minds keep us distracted from paying attention to our inner guidance that nudges us this way instead of that way. We rarely pay attention to that little voice inside, your intuitive mind; it is the ego that drowns out the soft voice of your inner guidance.

You may often find yourself feeling as if everything is a struggle. Struggling to make things happen "out there" and wondering why it has to be so difficult. We have been conditioned to look outside of ourselves for everything. When we change our thinking (quieting the mind so we can hear our inner guidance), struggle dissolves away and allows our inner wisdom to guide us and bring our inner desires to us effortlessly.

THE POWER OF THE CONSCIOUS
AND SUBCONSCIOUS MINDS

The ego is interesting. It is connected deeply to the conscious mind, our left brains. It represents no more than 10 percent of our mental potential, which is just the tip of the iceberg. In the human experience, we have been conditioned to invest a great deal in the analytical ego mind.

The main function of the conscious mind is to think, and (despite popular belief) it can only hold one thought at a time and has no memory. The conscious mind's functions are to identify the two million bits of incoming information we experience every day. This part of the mind has a very comprehensive thought system around all of your perceptions of the world based on your belief system about yourself.

Ego believes you are separate from all that is – and it seems so when you look in the mirror. This sets us up in the world for duality: us and them, mine and yours, good and bad, and so forth. This thinking is destructive. The ego is traditionally in religion called sin, which is the term for violating ourselves or someone or something else for our own benefit. Many think the ego is who we are as people. If we provide the illusion to the outside world of our status with things, we may somehow magically become what we believe internally.

The ego's main purpose is to build, maintain and protect what it believes it to be. Some even think this is where self-worth lies. In reality all that any of us are searching for is simply love in our lives. Sometimes we use misdirected thinking – it's the outside illusion that will bring love to us. Whenever you look outside of yourself for anything it will not last. You will always want more and more to fill the emptiness because everything outside of yourself is only an illusion you have created.

In the work I do, the more separated my clients feel from their Higher Power, God or Divine Spirit, the more they suffer with feelings of fear, isolation, loneliness, guilt, blame and unhappiness. You are not your ego! You are not separate from all that is – and remember it's all an "inside job" as they say. You cannot find love outside of yourself. True love comes only from within, and you will attract no more from the outside than you already have within. We have simply mistaken who our master is.

The function of your subconscious mind is to *store and retrieve the information provided to it*. It does not know real from unreal. Its job is to ensure that you respond exactly the way you have been programmed throughout your life (remember, 80 percent by age eight!). The subconscious mind has merely accepted most of what you now consider to be your core belief system, as it has no ability to reason, discern or attach meaning or value to it up until the age of eight. Your subconscious mind takes everything you say and do fit a pattern consistent with how you perceive yourself to be and wants you be right and safe in those perceptions even if it causes pain.

The right mind is deeply connected to the heart, and its core lessons are forgiveness. Only love is real. Everything else is an illusion that we call fear. When you begin to live from this deeper level of love and forgiveness and clear out what no longer serves you, this is where you can begin to heal and release pain that you thought was yours to carry in life. Do you really want the pain from the illusion that ego has provided?

When you practice forgiveness you automatically open to love, which is what we are all ultimately striving to experience more and more of. Remember, forgiveness is not condoning what someone has done or said to you. It is releasing the emotional charge it has around the action thereby releasing you energetically so it no longer causes harm thereby setting you free. Just because you forgive someone doesn't mean you have to go to lunch with them. It simply means you've let it go. If we can only look for the lesson in whatever has happened we can then clearly see the purpose for us to have experienced that particular situation. We can then become empowered by it as opposed to being a victim of it, thereby releasing our self from the bondage it created. You are the only one thinking in your mind. You have the ability to change what and how you are thinking. This ability provides simple choices so your highest purposes can be fulfilled.

I remember many years ago I went to an astrologer (his name has long ago left my memory). However, I remember sitting in his office across from this man in a large leather chair, sitting behind a large desk and a bookshelf that spanned the wall behind him full of books. He said something to me that changed my life forever. I remember nothing else of this reading other than he said, "Jesus forgave you, why can't you forgive you?"

If you could actually see a mind-shift you would have seen it in me that day. No matter your religious views, most will agree that the Christian viewpoint is that Jesus died for our sins and forgave us. I remember thinking, yes I have been forgiven. Up until that moment I had put myself above this enlightened being (Jesus) who had so selflessly taken this burden from me. I had never really thought about this idea before that day even though I was raised in a religion that spoke of this. The key is I never truly thought about this concept or to this depth. I realized that before this profound statement I had just accepted that I had no right to let go of this stuff in my own life, it was mine to carry, I had to pay for all the wrong I've done, I didn't even think or know up until that moment I had a choice to let it go and that I didn't deserve to carry these burdens as self punishment any longer. How about you?

This is ego at its finest. So many of us carry burdens that are not meant to be carried. We all have experiences in life that we hold regret around. We use self-punishment, self-loathing, self judgment, well you know the drill right! We are much harder on our self than anyone else in the end. There was someone in my life that I was angry and unforgiving toward. After doing some work around it I realized I had pretty much forgiven them, it was me that I couldn't forgive or let go of why I did or didn't do what I had done around the situation. Take a closer look so you have more clarity, these are the things great shifts are made of! Remember, the only purpose anything we experience has for us is to learn – and that is it. Learn from it and let it go.

We serve no one holding on to all of this fear. You only hurt yourself. Release all that needs to be released so you can experience the essence of what love truly is and make a stronger connection to your Divine Energy. You've already been forgiven, and now you just need to learn how to forgive yourself and others in the truest sense.

I believe it is your birthright to be happy, prosperous, abundant, joyful, purposeful and live life the way you desire from the highest vista you can imagine. We have all been sold a bill of goods by the ego mind that we must be a slave to money, and that life is not meant to truly be lived to its fullest. We subscribe to ideas that we should be ruled by negative emotions and allow others to rule over us, to fear life, to fear our self and give our power away. It is up to us to change our beliefs of lack and duality so we can heal at last and wake up to who we are and embrace our true selves. Simply, Awaken to Heal!

"You are a brilliant, powerful light who can create in loving beautiful ways that serve all."

You literally create the state of your health by your beliefs and thoughts. Most health issues we deal with stem from how we think. For example, anxiety, panic, PTSD (Post Traumatic Stress Syndrome), stress (which has now been deemed a medical condition because it's so rampant and is the basis for 90% of health issues) is all caused around fear of the future whether it stems from trauma, lifestyle or our programming. Depression is getting stuck in the past, i.e. we are not fully expressing in our life and most people experiencing one have symptoms of both, for example panic and depression. They are literally having extreme trouble finding the present moment fully. I understand that trauma is no small matter yet by slow, careful, conscious work and removing blocks (which accelerates the process) around events that caused it (without necessarily reliving the past) you can move through these experiences. It's like either being stuck in or *moving through* the "black hole," you can emerge from these states with new insights, understandings and lessons that will support you the rest of your life.

We have forgotten how to live in the moment and discern what we want in our lives and what we don't want. We allow ego to rule us and keep us in fear. For most of us the left-brain is more highly developed than the right hemisphere, and we need tools now to learn to integrate the conscious mind with the subconscious mind so we can follow our deep inner guidance. The answers you search for will never come when the mind is busy, they will only come when the mind is quiet.

You will know when these two minds have merged and become more integrated because life will be working more easily. You'll feel like you're in "the flow of all that is good" instead of feeling like life is a struggle. The key is to get rid of all the rubbish accumulated and remove the blocks and obstacles. When you can accomplish these tasks you'll feel like you've taken a deep breath of fresh air for the first time and you'll never want to go back to the struggle again.

When you realize that loud, obnoxious, analytical talk you hear constantly isn't even your voice, it's the voice of parents, guardians, teachers, or extended family members who have input their old patterns into you without you being able to do anything about it you'll begin to pay attention! Remember, 80 percent of your core programming was done by the age of eight, and for the most part we run around like grown-up eight-year-olds with these thoughts and beliefs and wonder why life isn't working the way we wish that it would. It's time to break free! We need to take responsibility for what we want in our lives and what we don't want.

The conscious mind now may decide it's time to make changes. The only problem is all of the old programming and recordings that you've accepted are buried deep in the unconscious. You may feel without those old ideas, values or beliefs you may not know who you are anymore or what to do or how life will be or how you'll feel if you release what you believe is your truth even when it no longer serves you and causes you pain. It may feel a little disconcerting, maybe even scary like moving to a foreign country where you don't know the language. Our emotions takeover at the subconscious level to keep us safe, and all of those feelings of worry, doubt and fear rear their ugly heads and once again keep us stuck right where we're at keeping the battle between the conscious and subconscious mind active.

I saw this first hand in one of my PTSD clients. He wanted so badly to move past the PTSD at the outset because his marriage was failing and he knew he needed help. However, he didn't complete the program we'd set up, fell out of integrity completely with himself and me and what he'd committed to. I saw him later speaking to someone in authority and he went into his abusive childhood, fully in his victimhood, and how he doesn't trust anyone which really wasn't even what the conversation was about, yet I saw so clearly why he will never move past his pain. He received great compensation even though it may not have been fully warranted in this situation because of the sympathy he was able to create. Remember when you get benefit from not being fully responsible or accountable, there is no way you will allow yourself full healing, where would your support or sympathy come from and who would excuse you from negative behavior? Remember if you can't trust anyone, it's merely a reflection of your distrust for yourself.

Change is difficult to confront after you've lived comfortably or even uncomfortably on automatic, right? Yet you know you need to make a change in your life – things just aren't working anymore. This is where you get that feeling the harder you try to make changes the more difficult it is to make changes. You get that resistance between the two minds keeping you stuck.

Some people "think" that if they are not thinking every moment or analyzing and dissecting every situation that they are not in control of their lives. I have even had clients who believed if they were not thinking every second they would be dead. This shows you the power of the ego. It will be in control even to your detriment. We base our thoughts on untruths we've accepted throughout our lives and built on from our early programming, which allows you to remain seemingly comfortable in your increasingly uncomfortable world.

Andrew Cohen in his book *Evolutionary Enlightenment* says (paraphrased) that our job is to gain dominion over our egos and bring balance to the left and right hemispheres of the brain in order to evolve. We are moving into the age of unity and leaving the mindset of duality; bringing balance to the right and left hemispheres of the brain is of the utmost importance for the next stage of evolution to occur so we may see at last with one mind, one vision which I believe is our next evolutionary step.

When we heal the gulf between the minds we can then restore our broken relationship with reality and realize we are not alone and separate. We can then remember who we really are – we are individualized expressions of something much greater. It is said that humans have anywhere between 50 and 75,000 thoughts per day. If we are not in control of our thoughts they control us, which gives our power to our old programming. Become the gatekeeper of your thoughts and no longer allow into your mind that which is not serving you for greater, expansion, awareness and the experience of love which we all desire.

Old programming is mostly from what we recorded as truth between 0-7 years of age, and now science has proven that we are also influenced by what happened in our mother's womb before birth. Fifty percent of our programming is complete by the age of five and another 30 percent is completed by the age of eight. If ancient sages and enlightened beings who have shared information, wisdom and insight are right then we may also bring in influence from other multi-dimensional times and other lives. All is possible even what we don't know or fully understand.

RESPONSE VS. REACTION

Many ancient texts support the aspiration of seeing with a "single eye" or "one mind". It is time as conscious-evolving human beings to do the most important work we have before us – and that is to find the truth of ourselves and realize our true power and to recognize the light that we are. A *reaction* is when little if any thought about our actions is taken; a *response* is when we become conscious and thoughtful about our actions; we become "response-able". When we respond in life versus react; when we choose with every thought what is best for us energetically to be thinking and our actions follow – then we are empowered. We remain a victim when we remain unconscious and at the mercy of our own misunderstood reactions.

No matter what your belief system is, this very moment is the most important moment. Yesterday is gone, tomorrow hasn't happened, all we have is this very moment. No matter what has gone before us; what has happened to us; how we were raised; or what we think about all of this, this very moment gives us the opportunity to choose again and think differently. Choose now how your future will unfold and no longer accept being a victim of the past. Claim your personal power and shine the light of who you are brightly.

We all have our personal future and the future of humanity literally at our fingertips based in every thought and choice we make. With your every thought you create something – and every thought takes shape and creates form. Just think about the chair you are sitting in, someone thought of it first (intangible energy), then made a written plan, gathered everything needed to put it together, and finally created the final product you are sitting in. It's no different if you hold the poison of anger in your mind (intangible energy). When you hold this emotion for long periods of time, chances are it will affect the function of your liver in adverse ways – and because the liver is part of the whole body, other systems are affected as well. Whether it's consciously or unconsciously that same energy also emanates outward to others – and they receive it on one level or another.

You are not bits and parts as the medical system would like you to believe. We are intricately created beings, and all parts affect all other parts to some degree or another. We are simply amazing and miraculous whole, complete and perfect beings just as we are.

If we choose to stay in victimhood, we are stuck in ego and negative identities that give away our power to a situation or someone who did something to us and feelings of helplessness in general. The difference between victimhood and self-empowerment is simply how we choose to think or perceive of any given thought or situation. When you choose to find the unique message that event holds for you for your growth and expansion, and you choose to release the negative emotional charge around it and practice forgiveness you become free and empowered.

Many of us blame our parents, spouses, children, bosses and on and on for one thing or another. However if you can look at yourself honestly and say, "All in all I'm okay," then it would stand to reason that forgiveness and letting go of all that has happened in the past is in order. The only thing the past has for us is to teach us – that's it. When we reach that understanding, we can stand in the moment and be accountable for our choices right now. This accountability is an amazing feeling of self-empowerment. You can let it all go and begin to create your life in a new way.

> *"The past is our teacher, the future our inspiration, the moment is our present…"*

If you have a label for yourself, you limit yourself, which puts you in a box of limitations whether those limits are based on a medical diagnosis, financial bracket, or ideas about what you can achieve in the world. You may also label yourself within family status, thought patterns, ways of eating, or other habit patterns that are all affecting your health and well-being – and much of this can ultimately create disease and imbalances of all sorts and stop you in your tracks from progressing, growing and expanding your awareness. Write down all of your labels for yourself and take a look at how, why and where you are limiting yourself because of them.

Labels or diagnosis can be of service in the short term to help you *move through* something. However, it becomes detrimental when you claim it as yours dropping into the subconscious over and over making it very difficult to break free from or heal from.

REPEATING AND BREAKING PATTERNS AND HABITS

Maybe you allow preconceived notions to influence your thought process. Maybe you have heard all the statistics you think might define you. For example, you could think you might already be overweight based on statistics and family history of obesity. Maybe you've heard about the numbers and chances of getting diseases like heart disease, cancer or high cholesterol – and maybe you falsely believe you could acquire these diseases based on those figures.

Reality is not the numbers or a predisposition. Your risk factors are actually based more on ways of thinking you accepted as yours from those close to you, your lifestyle and practices adopted from family (for example obesity or other disease based on the lifestyle you're repeating). You're not doomed. It's time to become aware and to make changes in regard to your family's lifestyle, eating habits, thought patterns and behaviors that increase risk factors. This even applies to relationships, money and how you manage emotions.

Take the knowledge of what has gone on in your family and make different choices: eat healthier, get an education on optimal nutrition, move your body to stay fit and lean. Maybe even understand the spirituality of eating and meditation that feeds your mind, body and spirit. Understand that you create health or lack of health by how you think, make healthier relationship choices, and more. You don't have to buy into the limitations that society wants for you. You can choose differently.

Allow yourself to release all of your negative identities and realize these are moments you are merely passing through, not a lifelong identity that keeps you vulnerable to repeat past behaviors or gives you excuses to stay right where you're at. It's time to get out of the box you have created for yourself. Realize everything is merely a choice. How would you change your story if you realized whatever you are suffering with right now was your choice? Claim your birthright *now*.

Claim your right to be happy and your personal freedom to choose all you desire in your life and live your life to its fullest!

Now that you realize that you have created all that you have experienced in life and become accountable for it, now you can begin the process of consciously creating what you truly desire and "dis-create" what no longer serves you. This is great news! This means you really are in control in a healthy, balanced way. Anything that doesn't look so pretty in our lives has all happened for a reason. Now all we have to do is learn and move on.

You may say why would I choose "this" in my life? Well, I would say when you approach the *why* by asking yourself first *what* did I learn about myself or *how* did I grow from that experience because of this happening to me or from that experience or *what* am I learning now, you can begin to see the *why* of it. There's always a lesson if you only acknowledge it for yourself and then begin to live your life accordingly and *decide* how you want to think about whatever it may have been now in a different way.

Everything happens for a purpose, and that purpose is for growth and a greater insight and understanding of who you are. This helps us to forgive more easily and gives us the ability to move on from any experience with more wisdom and expanded thought and awareness. I believe this is such a beautiful way to move through life.

A WORD ABOUT RELATIONSHIPS

Your self-worth is not dictated by how others judge you or what they think you should think or do in your life. You may want to re-evaluate relationships that limit you – they are not for your highest good. Frankly, you do not have time to worry about what others think about you because that is merely their limited thinking being thrust onto you from their limited perspective; it's not yours. Furthermore, it takes up a lot of your time; time away from you creating your life in the way you desire. With practice and observation you will be more aware of what thoughts are yours and which are others that are of no concern to you.

Always go back to the inner truth of who you are; you know that truth; you know your truth. When others trigger pain in you this is your mind pulling from your history file, taking you away from the present moment which is your source of power and creation. Do you react or respond? If you've reacted you've then allowed your feelings to be re-created from your past painful experiences and then you may ask, "Why is this happening to me again?" You've then given your power to that person. When you respond you come from a place of "response-ability". Allow yourself to take a breath or two and speak from your truth gently, honestly and with integrity you will not have the same feelings of depletion as a reaction will cause.

> *"If you keep thinking how you've always thought*
> *you'll keep getting what you've always got."*
> **Dr. Michael Ryce**

Don't get me wrong. Feelings are meant to be felt. Feelings are your internal barometer. You do need a plan to bypass trauma or unsettled feelings that may be triggered by another person so you don't get stuck in them. Feel them, process them, learn from them, and let them go.

For instance, you may simply take a deep breath, state to yourself this is not my truth, use a thought-interrupt technique such as say "stop" or "cancel that" inwardly. (Thought-interrupt is used so the thought does not continue to drop into the subconscious mind and continue to solidify negative thoughts or beliefs about yourself so you can begin the healing process.) If you find yourself holding your breath this is also a way the body holds onto emotion, so become aware and begin to consciously breathe. Practice, practice, practice, it will become easier and very natural, and you will feel empowered knowing you are coming from a place of self-responsibility and love.

I utilize a technique in my practice of saying *White Light* until the feeling in the mind and body shifts, and until you feel yourself moving away from the upset, thinking more clearly, and experiencing the feeling in the body of it moving out. At that point I would encourage you to have some positive thoughts readily available so you can remember the truth about yourself, such as *I am worthy and deserving, I am loved, and all is well in my life and the world I live in.*

The full technique is first and foremost recognizing a thought, feeling or situation that has come into your awareness that you do not want; interrupt the thought (stop or cancel that), say *White Light* (building critical mass) until you shift the feeling, and then thinking something positive "in the now" is literally how you heal old ways of thinking and create new ones!

As you become more discerning regarding the thoughts you allow yourself - becoming your own *gatekeeper*, negative thoughts and situations will become less and less frequent. You will begin to live your life from a higher vibration with more and more awareness and responsibility and it will feel so good to have that type of positive control that you will remain in a negative place for less and less time (only long enough to process) and move on as to not cause yourself undue harm. This is empowerment!

Because feelings are so important we do need to feel them. Have a timer on hand and depending on how much you feel you need to release set the timer anywhere from two to five minutes. Cry, stomp, yell, punch a pillow, whatever you need to do to get all the negative emotion (sadness, anger, etc.) out and then when the timer goes off have a plan to shift gears. You may use the **White Light** for transition, and then go for a walk, take a rejuvenating bath or shower, read inspirational material or music, dance whatever makes you feel good and nurtured. Then observe any gifts of learning, and allow yourself new thoughts around the situation that caused any negative emotions so it is completely released and transformed.

Chapter 6
Health and Happiness

*The answer is how to get peace of mind,
feelings of comfort and happiness, and it is
something we all uncover for ourselves ...*

Did you know that we are the only species that has highly developed frontal lobes as part of the left and right hemispheres of our brains, which gives us unique abilities? These lobes sit in the front of the left and right hemispheres of the brain. The function of these two areas is to interact and influence our behaviors, emotions, thinking, impulse control, judgment, language, memory, motor function, problem solving, sexual behavior, socialization and spontaneity. Our frontal lobes also assist in planning, coordinating, controlling and executing behavior, even what we're going to do with our lives, and planning. It also has a great influence on our personalities, and who we are and how we feel.

Studies have found that the frontal lobes are involved in both higher level thought *and* emotion, and the implication is that we can use our thoughts to change our feelings in a very important way such as moving more toward greater happiness (and much more!), and we have the **ability to choose happiness.** The left side of the frontal lobe is more active when people feel happy. In contrast the right side of the frontal lobe is more active when people feel sad. When we discover what stimulates the left prefrontal cortex we can encourage or even train people to be happier from that stimulation. On contrast by learning what calms the activity in the right prefrontal cortex we can discourage or train people to reduce sadness and depression.

.As human beings our frontal lobes allow us to observe not only what is outside of ourselves, it also allows us to observe inwardly to be able to pay attention to what we're thinking; our abilities to make choices regarding our observations; our understanding and awareness of our feelings and more. This part of the mind is the seat of your emotions – the place where you are able to choose happiness, make judgments related to sympathy, feelings of sorrow, empathy, to be humorous, or devise deception, etc. Eckhart Tolle in the *Power of Now* calls this part of the mind the "silent observer".

Yes, you do have the ability to *choose* health and happiness! Many scientific studies show links to how we think, behave and react to ideas about happiness. Researchers determined that expectations such as, "If I make a million dollars I'll be happy," just don't work. In fact, it's quite the opposite. The cliché "money doesn't buy happiness" is true because happiness is actually the precursor to how we experience life, even our financial success for example. Financial success is merely an outward demonstration of whether we feel abundant and prosperous within or not. Happiness is undeniable and yet intangible. You project happiness whether it's in how you speak, carry yourself, take care of your health and appearance, and your beliefs about yourself.

So if you truly believed you had a choice in connection to your physical, mental, emotional and spiritual health, how would you choose now? Would you begin to live your life differently? Would you serve others joyfully? Would you choose how you could think more responsibly?

How would you choose differently? If you feel you have no choice and live as a victim what does your life look like?

Health is your wealth, physically, mentally, emotionally and spiritually – it is your ultimate treasure that assists in accomplishing all you desire in this lifetime. Each choice is so important, and it's a gift you cannot afford to ignore. If everything is a choice, what is stopping you from choosing only the best?

A WORD ABOUT THE POWER OF NOW

So many people are confused, have health problems, worship their egos, their bank accounts, and more. We somehow believe we are not worthy of being happy and joyful and must sacrifice important things for jobs where we feel enslaved to money, and many people fritter away their lives in quiet desperation for something more. The one thing in life we cannot borrow against, go back and recover, or change how it is dispensed is our precious time. Time is a precious and valuable gift. We all have the same 24 hours. All we have is this moment; this very moment where creation, healing and life happens.

When we live waiting for tomorrow then we are enslaved and possibly surprised if the tomorrow we were waiting for never comes in the way we thought it would. This can lead to hopelessness or settling for mediocrity. Regret is a bitter pill to swallow when life (our time) on this plane is running out or at an end.

I knew a man who worked at a grocery store I frequented for many years who had dreams of traveling when he retired, and he made many sacrifices. He finally retired and began to plan his trips he had so patiently waited for. Three weeks after retiring he passed away from a heart attack. I know you may have heard stories like this before, however remember life is to live now! Don't wait until tomorrow. It may never come. Yes, we have real responsibilities; however, don't allow them to stand in your way by putting off your purpose or your dreams.

"Life will invite us into it with a luring, with a calling, with an inner nudge. The greatest gift life made to you is yourself. You are a spontaneous self-choosing center in life, the certainty of eternal expansion. You are a limitless Self."
Ernest Holmes

THE PRACTICE OF BEING POSITIVE

- Believe it is your choice to be positive.
- Surround yourself with positive, loving people.
- Interrupt negative thoughts by saying "cancel that".
- Have positive affirmations in the present tense close at hand to replace any thoughts that no longer serve you.
- Use the *White Light Technique.*
- Become conscious of what you have control over and what you don't, and then lovingly let it go and make necessary corrections.
- Be kind to yourself and others. Practice the Golden Rule.
- Focus on the good in you and your life and more of the same will come.
- Share your positivity with others.

HOW THOUGHTS AND ATTITUDES AFFECT HEALTH

Ask yourself how you feel? No one knows you better than you. Make a list of the positive ways you feel in your life and the not-so-positive ways you feel in your life and you'll begin to see the picture of your feelings, where you are in balance and where you may not be and then you can make some new decisions. Your opinion matters.

A study at Duke University found when they asked almost 3,000 heart patients to classify their health as poor, fair, good, or very good. As reported in the *Journal of Medical Care*, those who chose "very good" were about 70 percent less likely to die within three years than those who answered "good". And they had three times the survival rate of those who claimed "poor" health!

Another dramatic example of the power of your perceptions was stated in a study of more than 5,000 people over the age of 65. Researchers at Johns Hopkins University found that a poor image of one's health, regardless of any other risk factors, roughly doubled the risk of death within five years. In fact, a pessimistic outlook proved to be deadlier than congestive heart failure or smoking 50 or more packs of cigarettes every year!

Depression and anxiety can fuel many illnesses, including heart disease, hypertension, asthma, and possibly even cancer and diabetes. They now say stress is a medical condition and responsible for up to 90% of health issues. A positive attitude about health can ward off mental distress and may help provide important protection against disease and imbalances.

If you believe and then dwell in the thoughts that you are depressed you will begin to feel more and more depressed because your thoughts will continue to create more of it. We attract more of what we focus on. An awareness of your thoughts and nurturing a positive attitude about your health can ward off mental distress and may help provide important protection against disease. Get to know and trust your mind and your body. Trust the signals you receive and then act. Trust yourself first so you can make the best decision for your care possible.

Our body only wants homeostasis (health and balance) and will work very hard to achieve that for us. If we decide not to eat properly, rest properly, or exercise properly it will become more and more difficult for the body to keep up and that is when more serious issues can occur after years of trying to retain balance. This is what can happen when we allow our selves to be "unconscious".

If your body becomes ill it affects all other aspects of your life, affecting the quality of your mental, emotional and spiritual wellbeing, and it prohibits you from living how you truly want to live, thus depleting your ability to maintain happiness and well-being. You are not separate from your body. The more separate from it you believe you are the less important it becomes to listen to the body or trust it. For example when the body is in pain the body is telling you something - it is out of balance and to pay attention. When you become more deeply attuned to your body in ways that are beyond the intellect, you will be more in tune to what foods you need to consume and how much, you'll be more in tune to how you need to move your body, what you do to care of yourself, and you will be able to sense impending trouble more accurately than any medical exam can do for you.

I worked with a woman several years ago who came from a home where her thoughts and feelings were not discussed. She found relationships full of abuse and control. She was overweight and depressed. She was ready to give up on life. We removed the blocks at the deep inner-mind level, got to the root and the cause of the disharmony she lived with, without her having to relive any past trauma, and gave her simple tools to last a lifetime. When she learned how to be in control of her thoughts, used the techniques in this book, utilized the **White Light Technique,** and really paid attention to being the gatekeeper to her thoughts and actions, she changed her life. The weight just melted from her body. She no longer allowed her thoughts to control her. She "stepped away from her fear," and changed her relationships and her profession so her highest good could be realized.

This woman is now experiencing happiness in a way that is amazing to behold, and so can you! Our thoughts keep us captive and rarely tell us the truth about ourselves. I believe the truth about each of us is that not only are we deserving and worthy; it is our birthright to be happy, healthy, abundant and prosperous and feel love every minute of every day of our lives. Anything less is something we are still in progress of shifting away from. Life becomes a journey of remembering we are here to find love, peace and comfort; to remember that love is where we come from and what we are made of. We are in the process of letting go of all that does not serve us and what was never our truth in the first place. As we remember this, we can change everything for ourselves and everything around us.

Chapter 7
CREATING ALL YOU DESIRE

Fuzzy Intentions, Fuzzy Results – Clear Intention, Clear Results

We all want to create something in our lives, right? It doesn't matter what it might be – whether money, healthy and loving relationships, life's comforts, a meaningful job, our life's purpose, great health, whatever it is you can create it! Isn't that great news?

LAW OF ATTRACTION

The Urban Dictionary says that the Law of Attraction is: *"The belief that positive thoughts are magnets for positive life experiences and negative thoughts are magnets for negative life experiences. Based on the Law of Attraction, if you have a specific desire and focus joyfully on that desire, it will be fulfilled.*

Simply put, The Law of Attraction is that which is like itself is drawn to itself.

Okay you say, how do I do it? The Law of Attraction is actually a real law of energy. There are many natural universal laws that we already accept easily without question such as the law of gravity, laws of planetary motion, law of thermodynamics, law of motion and others. There are also laws of vibration, relativity, cause and effect, polarity, rhythm, gestation and transmutation. Many of these are intangible yet we still accept them. The Law of Attraction is no different.

One little exercise you can experiment with is to simply sit quietly (ideally for 60 seconds). I call this technique *"60 Seconds to Harmony"*. Be very clear on what you would like to create, for example, *"I have $500 now!"* As you sit and repeat this over and over you will notice after a short time that another thought will come in to support the first thought and so forth. These thoughts provide answers and solutions and generate energy around it. This is a lesson in what we think we get more of the same, the Law of Attraction.

IGNITE YOUR POTENTIAL NOW
WITH THESE EASY STEPS!

Okay now let's get down to business: clear steps to creating in your life is to first have an **intention** in order to set it into motion. The definition of intention is: "The quality or state of having a purpose in mind."

Step 1: Create an intention.
What is it you want to create? What is the purpose? Why do you want it? Choose what your priorities are for now and make a commitment to them. How deeply do you desire this and what are you willing to do to get it? Write it down. It's valuable to see them on paper, and it gets all the words out of your head. Understand that intention is the first step it's the catalyst for everything that follows, the steps that follow will provide the outcome. One does not exist without the other.

Step 2: Be clear, detailed and direct.

Be very clear of each and every detail around your intention down to the smallest of details. Clarity gives you power and engages your emotions and vision. Allow yourself to quiet your mind so the answers come easily that you need and then write them out. Allow your list to be adaptable and then find clear physical pictures of your intentions and surround yourself with them. The mind sees with pictures so this is very powerful. Put these pictures where you can see them often throughout the day, around the car, office and your home, and visualize them as often as possible. Get clear, clear, clear!

Step 3: Take action.

We can't just sit back and not take the steps necessary to create what we desire. It just doesn't work that way. Taking action is imperative. Design a plan for yourself and stick to it yet allow for new insights on how to create what you desire. Realize there are unlimited possibilities for your goal to manifest. Keep asking for what you want in as many ways as you can think of. Always be open to change, this or something greater! Set your goals daily for tomorrow today. Each week choose a day to set goals for the upcoming week and each month for the upcoming month; and yearly for the upcoming year – and this does not mean to wait until December 31st. Your year can begin today! (*Use techniques and Resources in the back of the book.*)

Step 4: Create an unquestioning belief.

Create an *unquestioning belief* that it has already happened for you, never allow doubt or fear to take over or it will sabotage your intent and stop you cold. Remember the subconscious does not know the difference between imagination and reality so create reality through your thoughts so you can manifest your desires. Use **White Light** to move you through any negative thoughts or situations that may come up so you think what you want to think and not what you don't want to think. White Light will assist you to dissolve and heal the old neurological pathways of old thinking so you can now think how you want to think. When there is no thought or static, only pure energy between the intention and the creation, the left and right hemisphere, we will be creating as the Wizard and Magicians create, literally out of thin air!

Step 5: Feel deeply what you want to create.
Deeply feel with your emotions what you want to create; what you don't feel you won't manifest. Next, *get excited!* You will want to feel what you want to create and begin to live as if you already have it, visualize it often, and affirm it out loud that it is yours now. Sing it, speak it, see it. Always remember that you are creating this or something better! Feel appreciation and gratitude for what you already have created knowing it is already done.

Step 6: Remove the block and obstacles.
Remove and release the blocks and obstacles around all that is holding you back. Attain a qualified practitioner to help you dive deep into the inner mind to clear those issues that may hold you back from being successful. This opens new mental potential for all you desire in life. Utilize Self Affirmations to assist you in this process.

Step 7: Trust the process!
Trust the process of life, trust yourself, open your eyes to your creation, be ready for it, watch for it and expect it and accept it when it comes to you. Begin to live your life on purpose!

Intention = Outcome

Be aware that you may want to create something very much and start off in that direction, but also remember you just don't know what the big picture is for your life. We don't know what we don't know. We see only a limited view of possibility for ourselves. So part of your intention would include "this or something better" – and then be open and be observant to what that could be. Then "step away from the fear" if a fork in the road appears. If something new presents itself one thing you can try is to get quiet, ask for the answer, and then **trust** the answer. It's possible you needed to experience something before getting to that new place of acceptance and new version of your vision.

You are not the victim of the world you see because you invented it.
You can give it up as easily as you made it.
A Course in Miracles

Understand some things take longer to create than others so stay focused and in tune with your dream or vision – and it will come. There is a self-hypnosis technique called ***Drop the Thought,*** which you can use to enhance and support your creative process.

The healing state is that place between awake and asleep, and this is the alpha state. Many of us experience this state at least twice a day and usually more than that, between awake and asleep at night, and then sleep and awakening in the morning and also daydreaming are examples. So using the example of wanting $500 you will say as you're drifting off to sleep, "I have $500 now!" Say it once without analyzing it and then allow yourself to drift off to sleep (very important to do exactly this way). Always use the present tense, the subconscious mind can then get to work during sleep and dream activity to do whatever needs to be done or undone to create what you desire at the subconscious level. Again, do as long as needed until results are created, and then it's time to create something new!

A WORD ABOUT MEDITATION

Many years a go I was on a wonderful hike in the mountains with some dear friends. We took a few minutes out for quiet meditation in the Cathedral of Nature. A clear message came to me that day – and that was to *"Be Who You Are!"*

There is nothing more important than learning to quiet the mind so you can hear what your soul has to say and wants you to hear. Developing a meditation practice is extremely valuable. It allows the busy analytical mind to quiet so you can hear your inner guidance where the answer to every question you have is just waiting to be delivered to you. I encourage you to learn this practice. There are more than 100 benefits of practicing this ancient art.

It is never a waste of time to listen to your inner guidance. I don't know about you, but whenever I've not followed that guidance of that small inner voice or my "better judgment" I've lived to regret it every time without exception. Practice listening intently, all of the answers you need are within you just wanting to be heard and recognized. Trust you, trust your connection to the Source of All That Is, there is no greater lesson. You will never be led astray by your deep inner guidance.

"To the mind that is still the whole universe surrenders."
Lao Tzu

We are such powerful beings, and we are just now remembering who we really are again. We are unique and special. Your life is a gift. Even Jesus in *John 14:12-14;* "*I tell you the truth. The person that believes in me will do the same things I have done. Yes! He will do even greater things than I have done.*"

I love this verse. It's simply time to remember that you are not disconnected from all that is; you are connected in all its glory and an integral part of all that *is.* You have abilities that you don't feel worthy of even entertaining the thought you might have. It takes practice to become more aware. The secret is to begin now, to be more conscious, deciding what's all right in your life and what's not, setting healthy boundaries for yourself, living with integrity and honor for yourself, and learning to love yourself. Being accountable and responsible; being kind yet authentic with others; finding balance and healthy boundaries are all wonderful ways to begin finding your inner true radiant power that shines as bright as the brightest star!

Chapter 8
Expanding Your Light ~ Spiritually Speaking

"If you don't know where you're going,
any road will take you there."
George Harrison

Before I begin, please understand my point here has little or nothing to do with religion. My ideas relate to spirituality, a broad perspective of universally understood ideas. I would not be in my integrity if I did not open the conversation to this level of consciousness for contemplation. There is a saying that religion is someone else's experience, and spirituality is your own experience – and I believe it is much more.

In simple terms, spirituality is how you live your life in each and every moment. It is based on basic tenants and truths such as: treat others as you would like to be treated, respect yourself and others, live in integrity and honor, and be true to yourself following your inner truth and higher guidance. It embraces ideas that you are connected to something greater than yourself no matter what name you call it (God, Buddha, Mohamed, Spirit, Love, Universe etc.). Living in this way, according to these ideals and principles takes practice, perseverance and consciousness. Your intent would become getting clear with yourself and understanding the energy generated from within you is put out to others and into the outer world, which is a great responsibility.

Spirituality transcends your thought processes as well. It shows through in the ways you care for your body by participating in activities that nurture and enhance the body such as body movement and intake of proper nutrition. Do you consume the best foods from Mother Earth? Do you drink clean water?

A mindful awareness of these things also means you live spiritually. Even releasing your being of poisonous anger, worry, doubts and negative limitations will allow you to live a more mindful spiritual life. When you connect regularly with the beauty of nature in all its glory, you experience and live spiritually. When you allow yourself to be open to greater possibilities that are open to you and embrace your freedom and ability to be prosperous and abundant because these are your birthrights, you live spiritually. When you are open to all the gifts that are yours, recognize them, and then claim them, you live spiritually.

You are the only one who decides your limitations, believes in lack, and invites illness into your body. You are not a victim you are the creator of your life. When you become accountable for what has been created in your life, then and only then can you make changes and create something new for yourself. The difference between being a victim versus being empowered in life is simply a choice. Ignorance is not real. You create whether you decide to be conscious of it or not. When you decide to be conscious of your choices you will become empowered – and when you become self-empowered all possibilities completely open to you.

"Once you believe in yourself and see your soul as divine and precious, you'll automatically be converted to a being who can create miracles."
Wayne Dyer

A WORD ABOUT MIRACLES

Miracles are defined as *an event that appears to be contrary to the laws of nature or is amazing or extraordinary or even unexpected and regarded as an act of God.*

We are surrounded by miracles every day and in every way if you think about it. Miracles come in all shapes and sizes like spaceships that travel the cosmos (ours and others), or jet airlines that transport thousands and thousands of people all over the world. Miracles are often small, simple or even unrecognized. Miracles include conception, birth, the cycles of Mother Nature, and love between people or animals and cannot be touched. Miracles can be our ability to harness the natural occurrences like electricity or creation of transportation to take us to destinations far and wide. Actually the list is long if we sit in gratitude about all we have around us that make our lives lovely, beautiful or comfortable and remind us of high values and harmony.

The more we acknowledge the miracles in our lives however small, the more we open to more of the same. Who wouldn't love a few more miracles in their lives? Just look for them and you will find them.

"Every breath is a sacrament, an affirmation of our connection with all other living things, a renewal of our link with our ancestors and a contribution to generations yet to come."
~ *David Suzuki*

Making the world a better place takes consciousness. We're all responsible for what we think. Energetically it emanates out from us and not only affects us it affects everything outside and around us. I have been a part of energetic experiments where the energy of a human being could be read 100 feet or more away from them, and I believe it is further out than we can imagine for some.

How many times have you been told: "You're not the center of the universe?" This is not true, you are! No, not in an ego-centered way. Remember if you have the same makeup of star systems and planets, from what we know about our cellular and molecular structure of the body, then your body is its own universe. Thus, wouldn't it stand to reason that your thoughts and decisions control this vehicle called your body? You control your health, well-being and attitude, and therefore everything that emanates from it or is created by it. We are literally the Gods and Goddesses of this human body we inhabit!

Energy is energy no matter what form it takes. When you live in gratitude you literally open floodgates of more to come into your life, and it opens you to more inner peace and purpose in life. When you step away from fear and doubt and *live your life as an adventure* you live without anxiety. When you *embrace the adventure that is life* you will discover a freedom like no other. When you release the past you leave behind depression, regret, and undo the shackles that keep you stuck in unhappiness that forfeit your peace and resist the amazing choices you have to create your future anew. When you are in service to others you remove yourself from greed and selfishness.

You instead open to the grace of knowing all people are one, more alike than different. Humans are all the same in that we are all energy beings. Everyone is here to learn to love each other and to live with cooperation and harmony with one another.

When you begin to live your life from your innate truth you no longer need government or religion to define your belief system. You won't allow outsiders (individuals, groups or institutions) to control you. You live from integrity in whatever you do – and let it all come from a reflection of your inner light, truth and higher consciousness. As they say "truth will set you free."

Imagine communities where food and water is clean and pure. People are kind, gentle, cooperative, and live to support each other. It's being done in small communities, and it is possible for all of us if we just choose to make it so.

Once you have expanded your mind and begin to vibrate at a higher level and no longer accept old ways of thinking, there is no going back. You could never be happy in that old mindset again. You will also begin to draw people and new experiences that vibrate at these higher levels, which enhance and begin a new cycle of higher vibration allowing you to continue a spiraling of lighter and lighter vibration on and on ...

So open your arms to the future. See life as an adventure, embrace the adventure that is life, and know you can navigate whatever comes your way. You are strong and have the tools required to make it to the other side of this experience with the realization that nothing lasts forever as it stands, everything is always changing; we are just passing through. The only thing we can depend on in life is change so move with it, explore it, and have fun with it. Know all has come into your life to teach you something. Practice living simply, listening to the voice of your soul, thinking from a higher level of consciousness – and then happiness will envelop you beyond what you can imagine. When consciousness is raised one soul at a time then the world will change.

At the heart of all spiritual teachings are simple truths for us to become and express love, peace, harmony, compassion, and joy.

Chapter 9

*"There has never been a time when you
and I have not existed, nor will there
be a time when we cease to exist."*
The Bhagavad Gita

I have an exercise for you designed to put you on the right transformative path: Let me ask you to find within yourself that highest peak of who you believe yourself to be and who you truly are. As you're standing at this highest vista of all you can imagine, feeling your true self open, and spreading your arms wide. Now open your heart to the heavens. As you look all around at what you've created, the good and the-not-so good, allow a deep breath to permeate your lungs. Know this was all on purpose to teach you the lessons for this life you chose to come here to learn and experience, and all that matters is that you understand what you needed to discover. Now release the breath and know all you need to know, and that it is so. Allow yourself to see your world now in an uplifted, joyful way, in the way only your eyes can show you and smile and feel it in every cell of your body. In your mind's eye literally shift and change all that needs to change for your peace of mind and well-being, and see it done now. Just thinking it makes it done.

We, the village of humanity, live in a place that can be heaven or hell. Life can be harsh and unyielding causing us to build walls inwardly and outwardly to protect us. When life is moving sweetly and gently we may bask in the light. However for most in our village we never allow the walls to fully come down keeping ourselves always making current decisions from past experiences and keeping us stuck even when life is moving smoothly. We remain on guard even when we know that the harshness of life or trauma we've suffered may or may not return. Then our lives are blocked from being fully open to the present. Survival means being guarded and untrusting of the world and even our inner selves, our thoughts. We remain imprisoned by the past.

Some people have decided now in these times of change to let go and trust the process of life. Even when the results may not be known, they take a leap of faith. What is faith? Faith is simply "unquestioning belief". Human beings all over are just letting go as if jumping in the river of life and allowing it to carry them on their way, trusting that what they desire in life will be brought to them, staying open to those things or something better than they can imagine!

For example, maybe you've decided to quit your unfulfilling job. You're scared to death. Yet, you chose to *step away from the fear* because you now know there is something better waiting and you're willing to explore the possibilities for your health, well being and highest purposes for being here. You may have an idea of how your dream will work and decide to keep an open mind. You decide to trust the process of life, which begins to open to new possibilities for you to create what you desire or something greater than you even imagined could happen. You simply agree to release expectations of the outcome and embrace life as the adventure it truly is and believe only the best will come to you.

It is possible it will not be a smooth road to what you desire; you may feel as if you want to give up and question yourself. When you remember the pain you lived with and what brought you to the point of wanting and needing change, keep moving and trusting completely. Learn to say yes to all good things and opportunities and follow your instincts. The universe will sense your desires through your vibration, your actions and thoughts and begin to match energy. If you're still not manifesting what you believe you want, there most likely are some underlying thoughts or belief patterns that need to be cleared. If you are ready, place your intention toward your desire, feel it, visualize it, and move your feet toward it, and the universe will unite with you to create it.

Remember to always be open to "this or something greater" as we don't know what the big picture is for our lives. Always stay open and fluid. If bumps come along use *White Light* to move through it. Life's bumps will get easier to navigate, and you will notice less resistance and more flow in your life as you become more aware. What used to bother you will no longer bother you or will be less cumbersome. Instead of great highs and lows, you'll sail through life as if on a sailboat, sailing through life with greater ease.

When you release and let go of what has you stuck in life you will be an example for others. You will be part of the movement to raise the vibration of life on this planet. You will see more clearly what is not working and be an agent for a way of living that is in service to yourself and the village of humans, claiming our birthrights of happiness, abundance and freedom on all levels. Yes, it can be done if you only begin now.

You may in this moment not believe this is possible. When you change your thought process and begin to live your life, as you know in your heart how it is meant to be lived, you will attract other like-minded people. You may even wonder where they have been all this time. You will then realize they have been there all along – it was only you who was unable to see or attract them because your beliefs and vibration were not in alignment yet. When you allow your light to begin to shine and stand in the amazing power that you are, you become a light, a beacon, drawing higher-vibration people and experiences to you. They are all light as well, and when each light shines brighter and brighter uniting, it is something that can take hold and radiate over the entire planet and beyond.

Continue to always step away from the fear continually moving toward love. Embrace the adventure of your life ever spiraling upward and outward mingling with the stars. We don't know for certain what is the next step in our evolutionary journey. I believe raising our vibrations, becoming the lights we are, and standing in our personal powers will assist us to get to that next level, which I see as simply the highest form of love we can imagine. What could we be in for if it's already as grand as that! Your efforts will not go unrewarded, be all you are meant to be.

I want to share a dream I had a couple of nights after the passing of Wayne Dyer who went to the next plane of existence on August 30th 2015.

I saw a vision of his head that was a beaming gold, halo of light that permeated his entire head. The message to me was that it's not really about 'going to the light' when we pass, it's about becoming the light, the portal so you are lighting your own way allowing you to move into your next incarnation or as Dr. Dyer said your 'next adventure' with clear memory of your past and taking it into the future.....

If this is a truth, then the only way to become that beautiful light that will light our way is to raise our vibration so we may *Shine Bright*!

So spread your wings, leap into faith, and trust and see where your personal journey is meant to take you. There is no glory in living a life someone else has laid out for you that is simply not honoring this gift of life that is yours. Live life to the fullest now. Be the best you can be, and your life will change forever bringing you great peace and happiness ...

It's time to let go, be courageous, and live your dream. There is nothing to lose. You know what you have, how has that worked up until now? There is everything to gain even though you may not know exactly what that is yet. Remember when you were five-years-old you had no idea what was ahead, however you bravely put one foot in front of the other, one moment, one day, one month, one year at a time to bring you to this moment. *Embrace life as the adventure it is*, allow yourself to accept it, because it is an adventure! Your perception of your life will change you and empower and transform you into the Power and Light you are meant to be.

Release worry, tension, fear, conflict, judgment, anger and sadness and accept fully peace, tranquility, courage, love and joy. Smile and experience nature often. Always remember we get what we focus on whether we want it or not so be conscious. Nothing can stop you from achieving your desires except you. Allow your light to shine brightly on your love and truth so your soul can continue to grow and flourish.

*When we listen with our hearts
we will find our voices.*

Final Thoughts

The Power of the Universe will come to your assistance when your heart and mind are in unity ...

And in the end you, your soul, which is the image of your spirit, your highest expression of your divine individuality and is connected to your Creator, will be the love, light and vibration you have generated during this lifetime. This is what you take with you as energy that never dies. That's it!

As Buddha said, "Believe nothing, no matter where you read it or who says it, unless it agrees with your own reason and common sense." You must experience these higher energetic ways of living for you to understand beyond the intellect. You don't have to believe anything I've shared either; however, if you have stretched your mind in the slightest and found new truths for yourself, that is all that matters. If how your life up until now has not given you the results you desire what do you have to lose to begin to think about and live your life in a new way? In an on-purpose way? Being conscious, joyful and grateful will open the portals of love, abundance and prosperity that are yours for the asking.

Learning to guard the thoughts and words you use is powerful for you and for those around you. Use your thoughts and words to uplift those around you. This will change your life and those around you.

When you accept life as an adventure moving with the flow of your life, trusting your experiences, knowing you have always been all right and always will be, and following your curiosity, you will be lighter, happier and live life without worry or anxiety. You are a radiant expression of love in the fullest sense – an expression of something beyond what we can imagine and grander than you've allowed yourself to believe. Honor your gift of life and know you are worthy and deserve of all the gifts of life you desire just by reaching out and claiming them.

Breaking your hold on fear and doubt, shining your light of love more brightly so you can live in greater harmony, being a catalyst for change and transformation in the way you know your truth and heart deeply desires, and then asking, "What else is possible for me?" Your will is your power to create all you desire. It is your nature to create and grow. This is our natural state. Allow yourself to know and feel what you truly love to do by expressing your purpose and reason for being here. Claim your gift of limitless possibilities for yourself and all you desire. There are simply no limits except the ones you choose for yourself.

Begin each day knowing it is a new day – a new opportunity for all that is possible and express love for your life. Allow yourself to observe what needs to transform in your life to bring more happiness, joy and light into your life. Not one of us is perfect, we are all merely in varying degrees of learning to find our way back home in our own unique ways. Be kind and gentle with yourself, and practice forgiveness moment by moment with yourself and others. Now, the question is: What are you willing to do to clear what blocks you from all that you desire? You are worthy and deserve all you imagine right now, are you ready and willing to just choose it?

Life is ultimately an adventure. There is little we truly have control over even when we think we do. Learn to ride the waves. Guide your boat gently along your journey. When we go with the flow of life and avoid resistance to negative thoughts and trust the process, we can experience more joy, peace and expansion. Open your arms to your future in this moment and say yes to all that unfolds and expect amazing things will happen for you.

Whatever you choose to do in life let it be a reflection of your truth. When you live from this truth, you will assist in raising consciousness not only for yourself, you will assist in generating light and love in your family, your community and the world. When you live from this example you will give everyone you are in contact with permission to do the same.

In the end there was light, vibration and sound. This is energy. Everything is energy. You are energy.

And love is all there is.

BELIEVE IN THE
POWER AND LIGHT THAT IS YOU!

About the Author

Linda is a Holistic Health Expert working and studying in this field since 1979.

She began her career in the Health Food Industry where she received an amazing education. Later she achieved a Bachelor's in Nutrition, and has studied and worked with many other modalities becoming Certified in Acupressure, Reiki Master, Yoga Instructor, Naturopath Specializing in Kinesiology, Feng Shui Consultant, Dream Coach and Spiritual Life Coach and more.

Her work has evolved over the years coinciding, yet not planned in any way, following the plan laid out to her at the age of eleven. Her work has moved into the energetic work of the deep inner mind as a Life Transformation Coach Specializing in Clinical Hypnotherapy. Her discovery of the true essence and power of who we truly are and how the power of our thoughts and beliefs can create and change anything in our life we desire, has changed her life and her work forever........

Linda resides in the Sierra Foothills in Northern California and is available for clients internationally. www.discoveryourpower.net

Printed in the United States
By Bookmasters